CU00929038

# The Bristol Deserter

## Alfred Jefferies And The Great War

## Geoff Woolfe

ISBN 978-1-911522-33-1

Bristol Radical History Group. 2015.
www.brh.org.uk ~ brh@brh.org.uk

# Foreword

The idea circulating among the labour movement before the First World War that "workers could have no interest in warfare but were to be the bastion of peace and international harmony in a new social order"[1] had, albeit fleetingly, some traction in Bristol. Ernest Bevin, then a full time official for the dockers' union in Bristol, called for Britain's neutrality. On 2 August 1914, at a largely attended meeting, Bristol dockers unanimously supported Bevin's resolution calling upon "the Government immediately to declare its neutrality in connection with the European war". Moreover, the resolution demanded that:

> the Parliamentary Committee of the Trades Union Congress, the General Federation of Labour, and the Labour Party... call a national conference to discuss ways and means of preventing this country from being involved in hostilities.

In moving the resolution Bevin said that English and Continental trade unions enjoyed a friendly relationship, 'and it would be insane to fight with them simply because there was a dispute between Austria and Serbia'[2]. The following day, in emergency meetings, the Bristol No.1 branch of the National Union of Railwaymen (representing 1,400 workers) and their sister organisation the NUR Women's Guild both voted against British intervention in the conflict and for neutrality.[3] This mood was reflected in the local liberal press prior to the declaration of war. The 27th July 1914 edition of the Western Daily Press warned that 'the whole of Serbia is not worth to us a grenadier, or to France a cuirassier'.

Once war had been declared on 4th August, the excitement generated was too much for some young men who thronged to recruitment centres to sign up to fight for King and Country. The rush to enlist had certainly been enhanced by a disastrous short-term deterioration in the British economy caused by the emerging conflict in Europe that summer. Historian Adrian Gregory points out that:

1 D. Geary, *European Labour Politics from 1900 to the Depression* (Houndmills, Macmillan: 1991), p. 31.
2 *Western Daily Press*, 3 August 1914.
3 *Bristol Evening News* 4 August 1914.

**Recruiting posters for the British Armed Forces in 1914.**

most traditional accounts of enlistment in 1914 have tended to overlook that the first impact of the war (and indeed the war crisis) was mass unemployment. Economic distress had always been the British Army's best recruiting agent and the slump at the start of the war was, in the short term, probably the most severe bout of economic distress in Britain in the twentieth century... Between July and September male employment fell 10 percent. [4]

Despite the common perception of immediate and massive recruitment, the vast majority of early war enlistees joined several weeks after the declaration of war. On 25th August 1914 two important events occurred that caused an unprecedented burst of volunteer recruits. First, the Government published exaggerated details of shocking atrocities by German troops in Belgium. The same day *The Times* published the "Mons dispatch", which gave distressing reports of the defeat and retreat of the British Expeditionary Force in Belgium and appealed directly for men to join up. In contrast to assumptions

4 A. Gregory, 'British War Enthusiasm in 1914: a Reassessment' in *Evidence, History and the Great War: Historians and the Impact of 1914-18* G. Braybon (ed.) (Oxford, Berghahn, 2003) p. 80.

of widespread naiveté amongst patriotic recruits, who supposedly thought it would be 'over by Christmas', Gregory noted that:

> Men did not join the British Army expecting a picnic stroll to Berlin but in the expectation of a desperate fight for national defence.[5]

In August 1914, aided by these fearful reports from Belgium and backed by decades of perceived threats from Germany generated by politicians and journalists, the British propaganda machine went into overdrive. From Poor Law Guardians to employers and Music Hall stars to Suffragettes the social pressure to 'sign up' was intense. In Bristol, as in many other places, a pro-war journal, *Bristol and the War*[6], was published that urged fit young men to 'do their duty' and volunteer for the fighting. Partly as a result of this jingoistic environment, Kitchener's now famous recruitment drive, which employed clever visual propaganda and, through the 'Pals battalions', insidious peer pressure to enlist, was initially successful raising almost half a million men in the first few months of the war.

However, the initial euphoria exhibited by large sections of the British working class, soon turned to anguish as it was realised that the war was not the glorious and righteous adventure many young men had imagined it to be. Reports of heavy casualties arrived from the Belgian and French battlefields and horrifically maimed and injured combatants were returning to Britain in their thousands. In Bristol, as elsewhere, it became increasing difficult to attract volunteers to enlist[7]. Alfred Balfour, the former Tory Prime Minster, addressed a recruiting rally at the Colston Hall, on 12th December 1914, but failed to attract many volunteers[8]. As one historian has pointed out, it appeared that "Youths who had stayed behind and ignored Kitchener's Call were determined to avoid going into Khaki"[9]. This would be latterly reflected in significant resistance to the introduction of conscription in early 1916.

5 A. Gregory, 'British War Enthusiasm in 1914' p. 80. Gregory's evidence is backed up by C. Pennell *WWI New Perspectives: Rethinking British Volunteerism in 1914*. See: http://www.youtube.com/watch?v=5W0657Bwn_A
6 Copies of this publication can be viewed at the Bristol Central Reference Library.
7 Kitchener's target of 92,000 enlistees per month was rarely achieved after 1914, despite the introduction of conscription in 1916. Great Britain, The War Office, *Statistical Abstract of information regarding the British Armies at home and abroad 1914-1920* (London: HMSO, 1920).
8 *Western Daily Press*, 15 December 1914.
9 J. Belsey, *The Forgotten Front: Bristol at War 1914-1918* (Bristol, Redcliffe Press: 1986), p. 27.

Many young Kitchener recruits were completely unprepared for military discipline and the harsh conditions they faced. It was not long before soldiers began to go AWOL or desert; the latter was an offence which could carry the ultimate penalty: death by firing squad. By the end of the war in 1918, thousands of soldiers had been convicted and, of these, over 300 were shot for desertion, 'cowardice' or similar offences[10]. They were mostly privates, from working class backgrounds.

Each one has a particular story, and now that it is easier to access official archives, as well as published secondary sources, it has become possible to fill out the details of their lives and their untimely deaths. The names of those who were shot were not generally revealed until the publication of *Shot at Dawn* in 1989[11]. Archives are, of course, only one source of information. Oral testimony and other evidence suggests that many other soldiers refused conscription or deserted, but they do not feature in official records.

This pamphlet principally considers one such story from the 'official' archives concerning two brothers from Bristol. The story of Alfred and Arthur Jeffries has been comprehensively researched by Geoff Woolfe; his findings and conclusions now follow.

Bristol Radical History Group 2015

## Alfred Jefferies; Deserter from Bristol

Official records suggest that there was only one Bristol soldier shot for desertion, Alfred Leonard Jefferies, from St Phillips. He enlisted with the 6th Battalion of the Somerset Light Infantry in 1914. No soldiers in the Gloucestershire regiment were executed, although several received the death sentence.

---

10 It should be noted that these are only the officially recognised cases, there are a number of accounts of extra-courts martial executions of troops by officers (and vice versa!). In addition, significant numbers of mainly black non-European labourers were shot dead whilst striking in a series of incidents in 1917. J. Putkowski, *British Army mutineers 1914-1922* (London, Francis Boutle: 1998) pp. 16-17 and 26-31.
11 J. Putkowski and J. Sykes, *Shot at Dawn* (Barnsley, Pen and Sword Books/Leo Cooper: 1989/99).

This pamphlet examines Alfred Jefferies' war story and the story of those with whom he fought and died. I also look at his family history and life and work in St Phillips at the turn of the 20th century.

I comment on the policy of death sentencing, how executions were arranged, the campaigning to reveal their extent, and the long awaited pardons issued in 2006.

I mention other deserters' stories, and comment about the political context of the executions, historical enquiry and whether we can be fully certain of all the facts.

# 1

## The course of the War and use of the death sentence

At the time of the First World War, the power to execute men for military offences was in the British Army Act, which was renewable regularly in Parliament. Execution for offences against military discipline was common at least from the 18th century.[12] The death penalty was of course, intended to be a deterrent to soldiers who were unable to cope with battle and army discipline. Anthony Babington quotes an unnamed brigadier:

> The execution of a man has a salutary effect on the bad and weak character...[13]

In the first stage of the war in Flanders, conditions were poor. Troops, especially reservists, were inexperienced and unused to battles in the field. Despite officers' warnings, many men deserted in the winter of 1914-5. Fourteen were shot between January and February 1915. Military police patrolled France close to the battlegrounds and there was surveillance at the Channel ports of Le Havre, Dieppe and Boulogne. As the war progressed during 1915 and 1916, casualties mounted as trench warfare continued, with shelling, gas attacks and machine gun fire.

12 See website article by D. E. Graves: www.napoleonseries.org/miltary/organisationo/Britain/Miscellaneous
13 A. Babington, *For the Sake of Example: Capital Courts-Martial 1914-1920* (London, Leo Cooper: 1983) p. 18.

By early 1916 there were 35,000 British army casualties a month[14]. Babington comments;

> when a soldier deserted… he might have put in jeopardy the safety of the men around him… panic on the battlefield can spread like the speed of light [15]

> Generals who had to make the fateful decision… were inured to the paltry value of the lives of the men they commanded. To terminate the existence of some remote and numbered soldier at such a time was scarcely a matter of great significance.

But, says Babington:

> Certain decisions to implement the death sentence … can only be regarded with amazement and horror.

According to him:

> Some soldiers were so utterly unsuited for military service, they should never have been in the army at all [16]

One man who was shot had been a vagrant in London. The medical board described him as having "a low level of intelligence".

Despite heavy losses in the early days of the Somme battle in summer 1916, Commander in Chief Haig ordered repeat operations of the same kind with more heavy losses during August and September. One infantry division were in a state of "nervous and physical exhaustion"[17].

During July and August 1916, 24 soldiers were sentenced to death and executed; 13 for desertion; 6 for cowardice; 2 for leaving their posts; 2 for assaulting an officer and 1 for murder. Many of those executed were suffering from shell shock, were exhausted, or were suffering from acute anxiety or

14 Babington, p. 56.
15 Ibid.
16 Op cit. p. 70.
17 Op cit. p. 78.

neurosis. Some had been wounded earlier in the war, like Alfred Jefferies. Nevertheless, the number of deserters was very small compared to those who remained at the front line. A colonel who had pleaded unsuccessfully for the life of a deserter in October 1916 recounted how he had seen the man during a heavy bombardment "hiding in an old gunpit and trembling with fear". His Commanding Officer, a general, said he should have withdrawn him from the line when he became aware of his 'cowardly' behaviour, or else taken disciplinary action.[18]

## The Firing Squad: Execution at Dawn

When an execution was arranged, a firing squad was assembled, made up of men from a different unit to that of the condemned soldier. In his book *For the Sake of Example: Capital Courts-Martial 1914-1920*, Anthony Babington describes the gruesome method used for execution.

> It was the practice in France for the officer in charge to load the rifles himself, putting live ammunition into nine … rifles and leave one as blank or unloaded

This was so that the soldier who killed his comrade couldn't know for certain that he had done the deed. The officer didn't have a rifle but had a revolver ready in case the soldier showed signs of life – then he would administer the *coup de grace*.[19] This practice was rarely used. The sentenced soldier was tied to a chair, post or a tree, and a bandage or cloth placed over his eyes. A white piece of material was placed over his heart to act as a 'target'. The order to fire was given by a prearranged hand signal… Executed soldier's bodies were buried in military graves and the headstone usually marked 'died'.

## 2

## The Jefferies Brothers and their Great War

Arthur and Alfred Jefferies were born into a large family in St Philips Bristol in the 1880s. Arthur was married, but Alfred remained at the family home,

18 Op cit. p. 56.
19 Op cit. pp. 45-46.

at Edward Street. They began their First World War service with the 6th Battalion of the Somerset Light Infantry In 1915.

Alfred volunteered in 1914 and fought in Flanders. Arthur enlisted in 1915, joined the same battalion as his brother, and they were in action together in France in 1916. Their war ended in tragedy, but in different ways. In August that year Alfred was reported missing from the trenches, and arrested by military police at Le Havre. Arthur was killed in action in September 1916 in the Battle of the Somme.

Alfred was court martialled in October 1916 for attempting to desert. He was sentenced to death and shot at daybreak on 1st November. He was one of around 300 soldiers to be shot in the First World War for desertion or cowardice.

Both brothers are listed in the Somerset First World War Roll of Honour Book of Remembrance in St Martin's Chapel at Wells Cathedral.

## Arthur Jefferies

In the 1911 census Arthur Thomas Jefferies was listed as labourer in a glass bottle factory, 27 years old and married with two sons. He joined the 6th Battalion of the Somerset Light Infantry and crossed to France on 28th December 1915. From July 1916 he took part in the Battle of the Somme. The fighting intensified during August, particularly at the battle of Delville Wood, and there were heavy casualties from enemy shelling. On 15th and 16th September the battalion fought in the Geuedecourt area, later known as the battle of Flers Courcellete. The war diary kept by the battalion Commanding Officer recorded what happened:

16th September 1916

9.45 a .m  Heavy machine gun fire from both flanks which inflicted heavy casualties upon us   and we were obliged to dig ourselves in without reaching our objective; further attempts to attack failed and at 6.20 p.m. heavy machine gun fire was turned on to us.

TO THE MEN OF ST. PHILIP'S MARSH
WHO FELL IN THE GREAT WAR 1914-1918.

| | | | | |
|---|---|---|---|---|
| A.E.ADLAM. | E.DIBBLE. | R.HEADFORD. | A.MERRIFIELD. | R.RALSTON. |
| J.ARLETT. | J.DIBBLE. | J.HEALES. | W.MIDDLETON. | G.RICHARDS. |
| T.BALL. | W.DIBBLE. | H.HERBERT. | J.MILWARD. | W.SEYMOUR. |
| H.BAILEY. | A.EVES. | L.HILL. | W.MILLWALL. | C.SHEPPARD |
| W.BARNES. | A.FARRINGTON. | T.HOLLOWAY. | H.MIZEN. | C.SLADER. |
| W.BATT. | A.FORD. | F.HOPEGOOD. | J.MIZEN. | T.SMART. |
| H.BESSELL. | G.FORD. | E.T.HULBERT. | G.MORGAN. | C.SMITH. |
| P.BEAKE. | R.FOX. | H.HURLEY. | G.MORRISH. | W.SMOKCUM. |
| T.BENNETT. | W.FOX. | A.JEFFERIES. | F.NASH. | G.STACEY. |
| G.BLACKMORE. | J.FRANCIS. | A.JONES. | S.NASH. | H.ST.JOHN. |
| W.BROOKS. | F.FREESTONE. | E.JOUXSON. | J.NICHOLLS | A.STONE. |
| F.BROOKMAN. | H.GODWIN. | W.LATHAM. | R.NOTT. | S.SYMONS. |
| F.BOOL. | F.GOSS. | A.LEWIS. | J.OGDEN. | H.TIMMS |
| C.CASE. | H.GRAHAM. | E.LEWIS. | C.PARKER. | F.THOMAS. |
| G.CHINNICK. | F.GRAINGER. | F.LOCK. | A.PEACOCK. | G.THOMAS. |
| F.COOKE. | A.GREGORY. | E.LOVE. | A.W.PHILLIPS. | H.TUCKER. |
| A.COOKESLEY. | A.HANCOCK. | J.MANLEY. | J.PHILLIPS. | S.WAKEFIELD |
| W.COTTERELL. | W.HARPER. | F.LLEWELLYN. | B.PITT. | J.WILSON. |
| W.COX. | E.HAYBALL. | O.MARSH. | J.PORTER. | J.WHITING. |
| G.DAVIES. | W.HAYES. | R.McDOWELL. | J.H.POUND | H.WOOKEY. |
| T.E.HULBERT. | B.HACKER | | | J.WAKEMAN |
| W.F.BAILEY. | | | | |

FOR GOD AND THE RIGHT.

**St Silas British Legion club memorial plaque.**

The attack again broke down with heavy losses. Our casualties were every officer who went over the parapet [20]

According to Everard Wyrall, historian of the Somerset Light Infantry, "The casualties of the 6th battalion in this affair were truly terrible".[21] Arthur Jefferies was one of 41 infantrymen killed that day. He was listed as a casualty in the Western Daily Press on 17th October 1916. 203 others were wounded and 143 were listed as missing. He is commemorated at the Theipval memorial, (Pier 2A), which is dedicated to those soldiers with no known grave and who were missing in action. [22] An "A Jefferies" is listed on the memorial plaque to those who lost their lives in the war at St Silas British Legion club in St Philips Marsh, Bristol. It is not known whether this is Arthur or Alfred.

### Alfred Jefferies

Arthur's younger brother, Alfred Leonard Jefferies was born in 1886. By 1911 he was working as a galvanised iron worker at Lysaght's engineering factory. At his 1916 court martial statement he said he had been with the 4th Gloucestershire Territorials for three years, based in Bristol, probably as a

20 From the Trench war diary of the 6th Battalion of the Somerset Light Infantry: mostly written by Captain Adjutant R A Somerville. At Taunton Heritage Centre; document reference DD/SLI/2/7.
21 E. Wyrall, *The History of the Somerset Light Infantry (Prince Albert's) 1914-1919* (London, Methuen, 1927) pp. 140-141.
22 Information on war graves and headstones can be found at www.cwgc.org.

part-timer. He then joined the 6th Battalion of the Somerset Light Infantry in August 1914, aged 26. His active service began when the battalion sailed for France from Folkestone to Boulogne on 21st May 1915.

The battalion's war diaries and the official file of his court martial[23] show what Alfred Jefferies experienced before he deserted. In their first week in France, the battalion marched towards the front line in Belgium. The hot weather made for a tough journey, and some men dropped out. By 31st May, the men were digging trenches to the west of Ypres. For much of June 1915, the battalion was under shell attack from the enemy. Around 19th June and again at the end of the month, they were under particularly heavy fire. It was during this time that Alfred was wounded in his right eye. He was sent back to the base for three months but returned to the fighting in August 1915. In September he was involved in attacks near the frontline in Flanders, including on the 25th of the month when there was a big 'push' that became known as the battle of Loos, in France. Many soldiers lost their lives during these two months, including at least four from the 6th Battalion. Their names are recorded in the periodical *Bristol and the War*.[24]

Following these battles, Alfred suffered from shell shock. He was in hospital in Boulogne from November until Christmas 1915, and then returned to his unit. In July 1916 the Somme battle began. 19,000 allied soldiers were killed on the first day and in subsequent weeks the 6th Battalion were engaged in fierce warfare, with regular exchange of artillery fire and shelling. This became a war of attrition with neither side gaining ground until late November, when the German army was finally pushed back, by just a few miles. During this time the battalion were in the trenches, being relieved regularly, and marching back and forth to rest camp in hot, muddy conditions. Over 100 men reported foot infections. 47 men dropped out of one march; 6 did not return. At the rest camp at Villers on 31st July, there was a shortage of water and a "lack of rope and buckets [for the well]". The men were reported to be "very tired".[25]

23 National Archive document WO 71/515 at Kew.
24 From *Bristol and the War* October 1915, p. 10-11; Bristol Central Reference Library. Two others from the 6th Battalion were also killed in action at Loos: Pte J Caines 21 from Broad Weir and Pte Frank Price 28, of 154 Church Rd, Redfield who worked at WD and HO Wills, Redcliffe St. He'd joined up on 2nd September 1914.
25 War diary as note 20.

CHARGE SHEET.

The accused No.9970 Pte A.Jefferies, 6th Service Battalion
Somerset Light Infantry, a soldier of the Regular Forces,

is charged with

When on Active Service, attempting to desert His Majesty's
service,

in that he

On 18/8/6, was absent from his Unit, the 6th Somerset Light
Infantry, and attempted to obtain a passage to England,-
his Unit, the 6th Somerset Light Infantry being then
engaged in active operations against the enemy".

Lieut-Colonel
Commanding 6th Service Battalion Somerset Light Infantry.

**Charge sheet for Private Alfred Jefferies at his court martial.**

During August 1916 both Alfred and Arthur Jefferies were involved in severe fighting in the Somme valley. The battalion war diaries record that the battalion went on a route march on August 2nd at 7 a.m. Orders had been received: "to get the men … as fit as possible in 4 days as we shall probably go  in the show at Albert shortly". They reached Albert on 7th August.[26] On 12th August, after attacks, the diary reads: "the smell is distinctly bad. There are still many bodies about mostly English not yet buried"[27].

Over the next few days there were more casualties of both officers and men of the 6th Battalion at Delville Wood and Montauban. There was constant night time shelling, and in the late evening of 16th August, there was an

26 As note 20.
27 As note 20.

attack of 'lachrymatory' [tear] gas shells; the soldiers wore goggles to protect their eyes[28]. Late that night that Alfred Jefferies went missing from the trenches. He travelled to Le Havre, where he was arrested by military police.

## The charge against Alfred Jefferies

Alfred was charged under the section 12 of Army Act that:

> When on active service, attempting to desert His Majesty's Service, … he: On 18th August 1916, was absent from his unit… and attempted to obtain a passage to England… his unit then being engaged in active operations against the enemy[29]

## The Court Martial

At his court martial for desertion on 9th October 1916 he gave evidence in his own defence to try to explain what happened. He said he was in the reserve trenches at Montauban on 16th August, and was warned to go on duty at 12.30 a.m., but at 11.30 p.m. he wandered outside the trench and was later:

> discovered by a working party of [the] Royal Welsh [who] took me ……. towards Brigade HQ on the way to Longeuval.[30]

On 17th August he went to the railway station at Mericourt, a village between Albert and Arras. He boarded a passenger train, but was not asked for a ticket, and arrived next morning at Le Havre. Here, he was seen by a clerk at the rest camp who asked for his leave warrant, but he could not produce one.

The orderly room clerk at Le Havre, who was from the Devon regiment, had been under orders to check all leave warrants, as only special leave was being granted. According to the clerk's statement, Alfred Jefferies was unsure which battalion he was in. He was wearing the shoulder badge of the Dur-

28 As note 20.
29 The National Archive document WO 71/515.
30 Ibid.

ham Light Infantry on his cap, and said at first that his name was Jones. The clerk said: "from the look of his eyes and his expression he was, in my opinion, mentally off his balance"[31]. He was arrested and taken back under escort to the battalion's rest camp near Albert, at Fricourt in the Somme valley.

Sergeant W. Hucker and two privates from the battalion gave evidence that they had seen Alfred Jefferies in the reserve trench during the day on 16th August but not later that night.

On the day of his arrest, 18th August, the 6th Battalion were under fire at Delville Wood and suffered heavy losses.

In his defence, Alfred Jefferies explained that he had been wounded, and had suffered shell shock near Ypres in September 1915. Two officers, Captain Adjutant R A Somerville and SM Cooper gave character references. SM Cooper said he had been a 'good soldier and was very reliable'.

As was customary for all courts martial in the field, the papers were seen by more senior officers until they reached the Commander-in- Chief's desk. Along the way, brigade and division officers could add their opinion. Alfred Jefferies' fate seems to have been sealed by a 6th Battalion Lieutenant Colonel who wrote on the file, above an illegible signature:

> No 9970 Pte A Jefferies has never shown much courage and has never been of any value as a fighting man. On the night of his desertion he could not have had any certain knowledge that the battalion was to attack 2 days later but I believe that he deliberately absented himself with the object of avoiding what he must have known lay before him in the near future. (Dated 10th October 1916)

### The death sentence

That same day, Brigadier P Wood of the 43rd Infantry Brigade recommended that: "the extreme penalty be inflicted". On 12th October 1916 Major General Couper, Commanding Officer of the 14th Brigade, signed the papers, recommending that the death sentence be carried out. He wrote that:

31 Ibid.

… there is no room for doubt that…. he absented himself DELIB-
ERATELY [original capitals] to avoid a particular duty…[32].

The file was sent to the Commander in Chief, General Haig, who confirmed the death sentence on 25th October. The sentence was rubber stamped on 27th October at 3rd Army headquarters and the papers returned for the execution.

## Shot at Dawn

The sentence was read out to Alfred Jefferies on 1st November 1916 by Captain Adjutant R A Somerville, and he was shot at 6 10 a.m. that day, in the presence of A L Brown, the Assistant Provost Marshall for the 14th Division.[33] The firing squad was made up of soldiers from the Duke of Cornwall's Light Infantry. A medical officer from the RAMC certified that the execution had been effective and the papers were sent back to Army HQ.

Captain Somerville's diary for 1st November 1916 reads:

Penin; 6 a.m. No 9970 Pte Jefferies tried by FGCM for desertion and shot just outside the village[34]

Later that morning at 7.30, the battalion held a route march of around 6 miles.

Alfred Jefferies was almost certainly buried at Penin village churchyard. Together with many other casualties who were killed in the Arras district, his remains were later moved to the large memorial cemetery at Arras Road at Roclincourt, north of the Somme valley. He is named on a headstone and in official records.[35]

The records state:

32 As note 29.
33 Ditto.
34 FGCM is an abbreviation for 'Field General Court Martial', held when on active service. Penin is a village west of Arras in the direction of Le Touquet and a few miles north of the Somme valley.
35 From www.cwgc.org/find-a-cemetery .The grave is thought to be no. 111 O 1. More information can be found at: www.ww1cemeteries.com/ww1frenchcemeteries/arrasrd.html and www.shotatdawnphotos.weebly.com/arras-road-british-cemetery.html

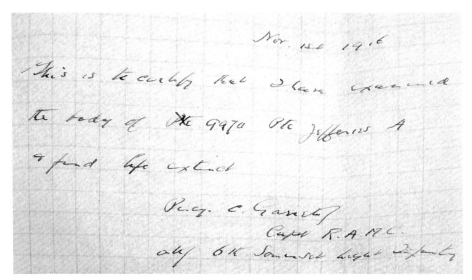

Alfred Jefferies death certificate.

Private Alfred Jefferies 9970
6th Battalion Somerset Light Infantry
Died on 1st November 1916
Son of Leonard and Georgina Jefferies of 33 Edward St Philips
Bristol
His brother, Arthur Thomas, also fell.

On Thurs 16th November 1916 the Western Daily Press reported Alfred
Jefferies' death with an accompanying photograph:

Private A Jefferies.

News has been received that Private Alfred
Jefferies late of 33 Edward Street St. Philips
has been killed in action. Much sympathy
is expressed

He was not, though, 'killed in action'. The official records use the word 'died'; as they did for all those
executed for desertion. As I discuss later, the authorities avoided giving information about deserters who had been shot in overseas action.

# 3

# Why was Alfred Jefferies sentenced to death and shot?

**Alfred Jefferies headstone at Arras Road cemetery, Roclincourt.**

About 90% of those sentenced to death for military offences in the field had their sentence commuted to terms of imprisonment. In this case, it is difficult to understand why this did not happen. Nevertheless, the attitude of officers, by their statements, suggests they were bent on a vindictive punishment, following a gruelling battle.

Captain Somerville's diary for August 1916 recorded events at Delville Wood in the days after Alfred Jefferies left the trenches. On 18th August at 2 a.m. the battalion dug new trenches near the Wood. At 6 a.m. British heavy artillery opened up, with the intention of breaking through the enemy lines. Instead, the bombardment fell short:

Repeatedly hitting our trenches and causing casualties… our men in the end became more afraid of our guns than the Germans…

On 19th August, the battalion were at rest at Fricourt. Captain Somerville wrote:

Our casualties were rather heavy; we lost Capt E D Parr, Lt E M Denton, 2/Lt W E Berridge, 2/Lt Davy, 2/Lt A C Pullen – all killed; 6 officers wounded ; OR [other ranks] 48 killed ; wounded and/or missing 220

On 21st August, the Battalion were assembled for the Commanding Officer, the Brigadier, [probably P Wood]: "The Brigadier had a parade and congratulated the men on their fine performance at Delville Wood".

Reading Captain Somerville's diary and the official court martial papers raise some questions:

- Why was the death sentence issued in view of Alfred Jefferies background of wounding, shell shock, hospitalisation and previous good service record?

- Why was the death sentence confirmed despite contradictory evidence?

- Were there no other witnesses who might have been called to support him and give evidence about his health?

It is reasonable to assume that the Brigadier Wood, Major General Couper and General Haig were keen to make an example of Alfred Jefferies. The battalion had lost many men in several battles at the Somme, and on August 18th took a severe battering at Delville Wood. It would not be surprising if officers and men felt angered when Alfred Jefferies reappeared, though under arrest, some days later. The record of the court martial suggests that he was not his own best defendant and found it difficult to justify his actions or account for his movements. Other accounts of the war suggest that this was typical for men under acute stress. The evidence of the orderly room clerk at Le Havre that Alfred Jefferies seemed "mentally unbalanced" is instructive.

Many writers, however, have shown that the legal framework of military discipline left little room for court martial judgements to be based on any civilian concept of 'justice'.

The 1907 War Office Manual of Military Law states:

> The object of military law is to maintain discipline among the troops ... while on active service, any act or omission which impairs the efficiency of a man in his character as a soldier must be punished with severity...[36]

This principle (punishment not justice) was embodied in the British Army Act. Records of Field General Courts Martial show how little consideration

36 This document can be viewed at https://archive.org/details/manualofmilitary00greauoft.

was given to the circumstances in which a soldier found himself before his officers, when he was under threat of execution. Field Courts Martial did not allow for effective legal defence, even after a requirement was introduced in 1916 that a legally qualified officer be present[37]. The system which resulted in executions was largely bureaucratic and ruthless.

Putkowski and Sykes in *Shot at Dawn* argue:

> Records relating to a number of these cases highlight just how arbitrary the decision to confirm a death sentence could be...[38]

They also suggest that junior officers were likely to opt for the maximum penalty. They say:

> To do otherwise was to solicit censure for lacking appropriate disciplinary zeal...and a dressing down from a superior officer [39]

Soldiers like Alfred Jefferies were considered by some officers to be 'worthless' as fighting men. They were arguably more at risk of being shot for 'cowardice' or desertion than others of more 'use' to their battalion.

# 4

## The Ultimate Punishment: Death Sentences in World War One

In 2005 a revised edition of a 1998 book by Gerard Oram was published which listed all the death sentences passed by military courts of the British

---

37 Putkowski notes that "the vast majority of the 304,262 courts martial cases that took place at home and abroad [in the British Armed Forces] between 4 August 1914 and 31 March 1920 involved soldiers and non-commissioned officers, of whom approximately ninety per-cent were found guilty. Two factors probably account for this comparatively high rate of convictions. The most obvious is that the courts martial were more preoccupied with enforcing discipline than granting defendants any benefit of the doubt. It was certainly true that most defendants would have been unskilled in their self-advocacy and unsupported in presenting their defence." J. Putkowski, *British Army mutineers 1914-1922* p. 10.
38 Shot at Dawn p. 12.
39 Ditto p. 16.

Army between 1914 and 1924.[40]

The list includes First World War soldiers who committed military offences under the Army Act like desertion, cowardice, discarding weapons and sleeping at their post, as well as murder, violence against an officer and mutiny. The list also includes those convicted of spying and treason, including James Connolly and other Irish republicans who took part in the 1916 Easter Rising in Dublin. Oram (p. 15 fig. 2) gives these figures for all theatres of war between 1914 and 1924:

|  | Death sentences | Executions |
| --- | --- | --- |
| Desertion | 2005 | 272 |
| Sleeping | 449 | 2 |
| Cowardice | 213 | 14 |
| Disobedience | 120 | 4 |
| Quitting Post | 82 | 6 |

Different sources give different figures for the numbers of soldiers executed on the Western Front, but the total was over 300 shot for all types of military offence.

Most death sentences were commuted to prison terms, often three years hard labour. Sometimes offenders were given (literally) 'fixed' (or field) punishments, such as being tied to a post for 2 hour stints for 21 days.

Around 40 per cent of soldiers who were executed were volunteers or 'Kitchener' recruits. In the Somerset Light Infantry, there were four death sentences and two men (Alf Jefferies and Louis Phillips) were executed. In the Gloucestershire Regiment, 26 men were sentenced to death, but all were commuted to other punishments.[41]

By comparison, in Germany, 150 were condemned to death and 48 executed.

40 G. Oram, *Death Sentences passed by the military courts of the British Army 1914-1924* (London, Francis Boutle: 1998/2005).
41 Oram p. 121.

France executed 600 of its soldiers (mostly because of large scale mutiny late in the War) and Italy 750.

If a soldier was reported absent, an inquiry was held. If he didn't return after 21 days, he was declared a deserter. A photo would appear in the Police Gazette. If arrested in the UK the soldier would be returned to his unit and kept under open or close arrest.[42]

In wartime, courts martial were held near the battle line, known as Field General Courts Martial. They were presided over by three officers with a captain's rank or above. The sentence had to be unanimous. Until 1916, a legally qualified officer was not required. Since there was only one such officer per corps, many field courts martial were held without one, as in the case of Alfred Jefferies.

Each sentence had to be confirmed by senior officers, until final approval was given by the Commander in Chief, initially Sir John French and later Field Marshal Douglas Haig.

The first soldier executed for desertion in World War One was Thomas Highgate, a teenage private from Ireland. He was sentenced on 6th September 1914 and shot on 8th September, just one month and four days after the declaration of war.

## Private Louis Phillips of the 6th Battalion

The court martial of Private Louis Phillips of the 6th Battalion of the Somerset Light Infantry illustrates the rough 'justice' of the process.

On August 8th 1915 he was found guilty of desertion from Ypres and sentenced to death, only ten days after his absence was noticed. The court martial file has this comment:

> The Court however put forward a strong recommendation for mercy owing to the mental worry under which the accused was suffering[43]

42 Putkowski/Sykes pp. 13-14.
43 The National Archive, Field General Court Martial file (Louis Phillips) WO/71/430.

The two officers who later decided the fate of Alfred Jefferies also condemned Louis Phillips to death.

The sentence was agreed by Brigadier General P. Wood of the 43rd Brigade, but he ignored the recommendation for clemency. This action was compounded by Commander of the 14th Division Major General Couper who wrote on 12th August:

... I can see no extenuating circumstances in this case

Four days later the execution was confirmed and Louis Phillips was shot by firing squad. As the note on the file by Lieutenant Morton of the RAMC put it:

I certify that…. life was extinct at 4.20 am on 19th August 1915.

Louis Phillips (also known as Lewis R Phillips) was 23 when he was shot. The battalion had been engaged in the Ypres area. Records suggest he may have been a barber from Tottenham; he was Jewish. He is commemorated at the Perth war grave cemetery (known as the China Wall) in Belgium near Zillebake. There is a Star of David on his headstone.[44]

Lance Corporal George Taylor of the 6th Battalion remembered Louis Phillips when he spoke of the War. His memories are included in Chris Howell's book *No Thankful Village*. [45]

There was another poor devil in our battalion what got executed …... A Jewish lad. Come up from the East End, up in London. Poor sod probably couldn't understand what we yokels were on about half the time. Anyway when we first got out to France we had a hell of a time of it – took a hell of a battering. The first day the battalion was ever in the trenches we had four killed, and about a week later Jerry started slingin' fire over and – guess what- it was us what copped it. Baptism of fire... Well after about a month of this the London lad were lonely or … scared or both and he runned away… He were caught … and done for desertion. Court Martial

44 Shot At Dawn refers to Louis/Lewis Phillips, but records his birthplace as Caistor in Lincolnshire.
45 C. Howell, *No Thankful Village* (Bath, Fickle Hill: 2002) p. 132.

reckoned he had good reason to be upset and that they should show him mercy. But he didn't get none. They shot he, too. Had to set an example they reckoned. I dunno. Poor lad.

# 5

## British Army mutinies in France

Mutineers were liable to the death penalty, but mutiny in the British Army on the Western Front was on a small scale compared to Russia, France and Germany.

Two days before Alfred Jefferies deserted at the Somme, over 60 men being held at the military prison camp at Blargies (near Rouen) mutinied. Soldiers confined there were kept in leg irons. Use of the latrines was restricted to fifteen minutes a day between 1.15 pm and 1.45 pm. Complainers were punched in the ribs; some were blindfolded. On 14th August, the men refused to go on parade. They were handcuffed and the ringleaders arrested. Six were court martialled and sentenced to death, but four had their punishment commuted to prison terms of between two and fifteen years. The other two mutineers, Gunner William Lewis, of the Royal Field Artillery, and Jack Braithwaite, of the New Zealand Regiment, were shot on 29th October 1916.

The year of the Blargies mutiny and the great carnage at the first Battle of the Somme tested the resolve of the military high command. As losses increased and troops literally bogged down, discipline became more and more important. Oram suggests that death sentences were more likely in the days before a major attack, when some soldiers might have been tempted to flee. As zero hour approached before July 1916, there were more desertions.

In 1917, a similar mutiny to that at Blargies occurred at Etaples base camp near Boulogne. Oppressive conditions there gave rise to violent disorder in the streets beyond the camp. Refusal to obey orders resulted in several arrests and courts martial, followed by the transfer of the camp commander. As far as can be determined, only one Etaples mutineer was sentenced to death and executed. He was former miner and Northumberland Fusilier Corporal Jesse Short, shot on 4th October 1917. Some writers, including

Allison and Fairley (1979)[46] have argued that the mutineers were motivated by sympathy for the revolution in Russia that spring.[47]

# 6

## Hiding the truth about the executions: questions in Parliament

It is clear from accounts of parliamentary debates (as described by Babington) that there was a sustained policy of denial and censorship in revealing the extent and details of field executions. This may have been a deliberate policy to hide the extent of executions or a means of sparing relatives the anguish and shame that may have occurred.

At the same time, serving soldiers knew the facts; execution would otherwise not have acted as a deterrent. Babington suggests that many officers felt little remorse at the death sentences when faced with some victims of disturbed or working class backgrounds with inadequate personal resources to defend themselves. Attitudes to mental illness and trauma have of course generally improved significantly in the last 100 years.

As early as June 1915 questions began to asked in the House of Commons about the extent of executions.[48] A Minister refused to give any information because "it was not in the public interest" but said that relatives had been informed. Some parents began to ask for more details and further questions were asked with the same perfunctory replies.

Labour MP Philip Snowden who opposed the continuation of the war, posed a series of parliamentary questions in 1916. He wanted to know how many soldiers had been executed. The Under Secretary of State for War replied that none had been shot in the UK, and again refused to give an answer about those shot overseas as not being in the public interest. He added "but I will ask my honourable friend to be good enough not to believe that the number has been considerable"[49]

46 W. Allison and J. Fairley, *The Monocled Mutineer* (London, Quartet Books: 1979, reprint 1986).
47 Both Babington (pp. 130-5) and Putkowski/Sykes (pp. 200-202) give more information about the Blargies mutiny and Jesse Short.
48 See Chapter 7 of Babington.
49 Babington pp. 66-67.

## Parliamentary efforts to change the death penalty law

A parliamentary report into the executions in April 1920 concluded that there had been no injustice. The report opposed the idea of a right of appeal to a civil court following a court martial death sentence.[50]

Labour MP for Shoreditch Ernest Thurtle campaigned for the abolition of the death penalty for desertion and other military offences. He wrote a pamphlet in 1924 *Shootings at Dawn: The Army Death Penalty at Work*, after interviewing war veterans who knew about the executions. Babington states that many of them were motivated by a sense of injustice and what they saw as the barbarity of the shootings.[51]

Thurtle had himself fought in the war with the 7th Battalion of the London Territorials. After being wounded at Cambrai in 1917, he was invalided out in 1918. Because of inaccuracies in the informants' stories, his campaign initially fell on deaf ears. Notwithstanding that essential facts of the executions were true, it was probably easy for military minds and government ministers to deny the stories, and be 'economical with the truth'.

In 1926 Thurtle proposed in the House that the death penalty be restricted to treachery and desertion to the enemy, but this was defeated by a 2-1 majority.[52]

Two years later, however, the death penalty was abolished under the Army and Air Force Act for the most minor military offences, and in 1929 the law was finally changed to keep the death penalty only for treachery and mutiny, and therefore could no longer be used for cowardice or desertion. A rearguard action in the House of Lords backed by military top brass opposed this reform but the Commons voted for the measure.

## The Jefferies family and the uncovering of the truth

Relatives were not always informed of the true reason for the death of a soldier, and this was the case with Alfred Jefferies. It's very unlikely that the

50 op cit p. 208.
51 op cit pp. 49-53.
52 Babington pp. 209-11.

Jefferies family, including his mother, knew about Alfred's fate in the years after the War. Alfred never married and had no children. His brother Arthur had two sons; the eldest was Arthur Leonard, who never married, and the second was Edward George. A third son died aged two near the start of the war. Edward Jefferies died in 1961 and it's possible that he did not know about his uncle Alfred. In any event, according to David Jefferies, Edward's grandson, no one in his family knew about him. During the 1980s David began researching family history and noticed Arthur and Alfred's names together in a list of Commonwealth War Graves, and from General Register Office archives, confirmed that Alfred was his grandfather's uncle. David then took part in campaigns for an official pardon for all those shot for desertion or 'cowardice'

## The campaign for an official pardon

This document records that

Pte A Jeffries of the
6<sup>th</sup> Battalion, Somerset Light Infantry

who was executed for attempting to desert on 1 November 1916 is pardoned under Section 359 of the Armed Forces Act 2006.

The pardon stands as recognition that he was one of many victims of the First World War and that execution was not a fate he deserved.

Secretary of State for Defence

**Certificate recording posthumous pardon for Alfred Jefferies.**

Information about military executions began to seep out after the Second World War and the publication of *Shot at Dawn* and *For the Sake of Example* accelerated the call for a pardon. It was increasingly recognised that field courts martial were, at best, a rudimentary form of trial and at worst, the route to the ultimate punishment for those considered 'cowards'. The campaign was supported by family descendants and the Royal British Legion. Media coverage, including a BBC radio programme about London deserter Harry Farr helped to create interest in this aspect of the Great War.

When *Shot at Dawn* and *For the Sake of Example* were published, official records were kept secret. The field court martial files at the National Archive were not released for public reading until over seventy years after the war. Julian Putkowski and Julian Sykes were then able to publish names in the 1999 edition of *Shot at Dawn*. Alfred Jefferies' file was officially 'closed' until 1992 and Louis Phillips' 'closed' until 1991.[53]

Further pressure was brought to bear in the new century and in 2006 section 359 of the Armed Forces Act enabled then Secretary of State for Defence Des Browne to issue official pardons for those shot for desertion or cowardice. A copy of the pardon for each case is included in the court martial files. The pardon for Alfred Jefferies records that 'execution was not a fate (he) deserved'.

# 7

## Written and Oral testimony

The three main sources for historical research; official archives, oral testimony and journalism can each give a different slant on events. Each of these sources can be biased according to the perspective of the writer, recorder or speaker.

The 6th Battalion war diaries, mostly written by Captain Somerville, give much information about the battles experienced by Alfred Jefferies. The court martial file only gives a tantalisingly brief account of his desertion and capture. The record of his statements to the court may only be an approximation of what he said. From the file records, however, we can conclude that he had had enough of the horror of trench warfare, that he was terrified and just wanted to get away and back home.

The attitude of the officers is clear; in the need to keep fighting in the face of everyday danger, they needed to demonstrate that no one could show weakness. It's likely that many officers had also had enough, but needed to 'keep the show going'. At the same time, their evidence at the court martial is testimony to the brutality of the war.

53 The relevant files are: for Alfred Jefferies, WO 71/515; and for Louis Phillips, WO/71/430.

In Chris Howell's book *No Thankful Village*[54] George Taylor gave his memories of his time in the 6th Battalion of the Somerset Light Infantry. He was wounded in his left knee, and his war ended in the 8th Battalion at the age of 19 in 1918. He was awarded the Military Medal. [55] In 1911, Taylor was 11 years old living with his family in Midsomer Norton. His father was a miner, born in Clutton. His son also worked in a local mine, as a carting boy. He enlisted as a 16 year old in 1915; he may have lied about his age. Initially a private, he was promoted to lance corporal at the age of 17. His army discharge papers give his address as Excelsior Terrace, Midsomer Norton, which is close to the site of the former Norton Hill colliery. His recollections are a colourful confirmation of some of the writings of Captain Somerville in the battalion's war diaries. For example:

All's we were ever doing on the Somme were goin' over the top somewhere or other. Every month it were somewhere different. And then we had the big one when- we took Delville Wood on the Somme. We got a good hidin' there, but we got up and took the wood. We lost 53 dead and 227 wounded in less than a day and a half – an' I'll tell you who one of 'em were. Every night a chap used to come round Midsomer Norton sellin' oranges apples bananas and things. Shearn his name was. Well, I'd just taken four or five new men into the front line and there were Perce Shearn in a dugout and while I was there a German come up an' stuck a bayonet right drew'n. I chucked a bomb at Jerry an'ad'n[56]

He also remembered the Jefferies brothers:

Well I'll tell thee another 'orrible story! We had two brothers with us who'd never go nowhere ner do anythin' wi'out each other if they could help it. They were in my platoon, so stands to reason I knew 'em both almost as well as I knew meself. And they loved one another – just like brothers should. They stuck together whatever they were doin'. Well one day when we were at the front, Jerry put this shell over and put the older one of 'em clean out – he were blown

54 Howell, *No Thankful Village*.
55 National Archive First World War records; discharge papers.
56 Private Percy Raglan Shearn was killed in action on 18th August 1916.

to smithereens – you had a job to find anything of him. Anything. Course, the other brother were all shook up – ass you'd expect'n to be- and he ran away from it all. An' don't blame'n.

About six weeks later I were more than surprised when who should they be bringin' up but this young 'un, what 'ad runned away. He'd got as far as Boulogne and tried to get on one of the boats. They brought him right up past me an' I told him how I was sorry for him- but he weren't allowed to speak to me or nothin'.Then he had to go in front the Court Martial. And next mornin' he had to be shot. And t'were  the Cornwalls what done it – not the Somersets- but men from our own Brigade. They put he out the way. Wiped him out. Wiped him away. You won't find him in any regimental history. He ain't on no plaque nowhere. They made out like he never existed. I dunno, that do make thee think. Have you got brothers? Have you got sons? I have. I've got both. (Howell p131)

As we now know, Alfred Jefferies deserted a month before his brother Arthur was killed in action. But what happened was a powerful memory for George Taylor.

# 8

## The 6th Battalion of the Somerset Light Infantry:
## Charles Buss, the Clifton archaeologist and the Dad's Army actor.

The 6th (Service) Battalion of the Somerset Light Infantry (Prince Albert's) was created at the beginning of the First World War in August 1914 as part of Lord Kitchener's army of recruits. It was formed at Taunton and later based at Aldershot before travelling to France on 21st May 1915. The unit was part of the 43rd brigade in the 14th Light Division of the British forces.

The Somerset Light Infantry's total losses in the war amounted to 4,756 men, of which 849 were in the 6th Battalion, a high proportion of the unit. 619 were listed as "killed in action", 167 died from wounds and there were 63 unspecified losses. After the battalion had been decimated, it was amalgamated with the 8th Battalion by 1918.[57]

57 Everard Wyrall, *The History of the Somerset Light Infantry (Prince Albert's) 1914-1919.*

Hundreds of Bristolians enlisted with the Somerset Light Infantry, many in the 6th Battalion. The journal *Bristol and the War* included news of local soldiers on the Western Front and elsewhere. The journal published the names and the background of casualties. They included Private B. Smart who had been a miner in Kingswood and was a machine gunner. He was killed in action at the Battle of Loos in the autumn of 1915. Several other men from East Bristol were killed in the same battle. Private Edwin Butson from Barton Hill, was 33 and not married when he was killed at the Somme in August 1916. He had a succession of jobs and had worked at Lysaghts. He was wounded twice; his brother Gilbert had been killed at Mons.[58]

Two Bristol soldiers were killed on September 16th 1916 in the battle that cost Arthur Jefferies' life. They were:

Private Ham who had lived at Crown Road, Kingswood, and worked at Scaddings boot factory.

Second Lieutenant R Meyrick Heath, who was 27 and lived at Mortimer Road, Clifton. He had been to Rugby school and graduated with First Class Honours in Classics at Oxford in 1912. He became an archaeologist and worked on Minoan excavations on Crete. He joined the Universities and Public School battalion in the 19th Fusiliers before joining the Somerset Light Infantry in 1915.[59]

George Taylor's memories, recorded some 70 years after the war ended, include his story about an NCO who had upset the battalion in training before being sent to France. One soldier was disciplined and confined to barracks by a sergeant for disobeying instructions while on parade drill. The same NCO later joined the battalion and during an advance from the trenches, the soldier, according to George Taylor, shot him from behind, as an act of revenge.

The NCO was warrant officer Charles Buss, who grew up in St George, Bristol, and was the son of a labourer. In 1911 aged 31 he was working as an attendant at West Sussex asylum for the mentally ill near Chichester. He was married with a young son. As a regimental sergeant major with

58 *Bristol and the War.*
59 Ditto.

the 6th Battalion, he was awarded the Distinguished Conduct Medal "for consistent good work and gallant service". According to the official citation, "He set a fine example to those under him". He was 'killed in action' on 3rd May 1917, and was buried at Tigris Lane Cemetery, Wancourt, near Arras Northern France.[60]

George Taylor lived until 1991 aged 92, having gone back to work as a miner after the War.

*Dad's Army* actor and playwright Arnold Ridley, from Bath, joined the 6th Battalion of the Somerset Light Infantry in 1915 and fought the same campaigns as the Jefferies brothers in Flanders and in the Somme valley. He was injured in the same battle that cost Arthur Jefferies his life. He was sent home and discharged from the army in 1917.[61]

# 9

## John Lysaght and Co and the First World War

Alfred Jefferies was one of dozens of men who fought in the Great War who had worked at Lysaght's galvanised iron factory. The works opened in Bristol in the mid nineteenth century, making small galvanised ironware, for example buckets and baths. The company grew both in Britain and overseas. They made corrugated iron sheets for buildings, including small sheds used as 'houses' by gold prospectors in Australia. Their two main Bristol works were at Silverthorne Lane (the Victoria works) and the Netham plant at the east end of the Feeder canal.

In 1889 Lysaght's workers won a pay rise after a short strike, and a year later there was another strike over non-union labour. The company closed the works for the duration, locking out the workforce. Whilst the plant was closed, the company took the opportunity to change machinery and working practices, effectively breaking the bargaining power of the skilled workers and the union. The strikers returned to work, but some employees

60 National Archive First World War records.
61 For information about Arnold Ridley see: http://www.spartacus.schoolnet.co.uk/FWWridleyA.htm.

The Lysaght's Victoria works on
Silverthorne Lane, St Philips.

were not taken back.[62] Workers there benefited from a sick club, a library and a canteen.[63]

According to David Bolton in *Made in Bristol*, when the German army invaded Belgium in 1914, river supply routes to Europe for Lysaght's products were cut off. On 7th August 1914 a company meeting of 1000 workers at the Netham plant was told they would be working short time. According to company history, there was no protest, but the workers gave cheers for King and country. During the war, the company manufactured goods for the Government including products for naval dockyards.[64]

In first few months of the war dozens of Lysaght's employees and staff enlisted as 'Kitchener' recruits. Many joined the 6th Battalion of the Somerset Light Infantry, alongside Alfred Jefferies. By the end of 1914, 1,449 employees and 67 staff from Lysaght's plants in Bristol, Newport, Scunthorpe and Wolverhampton were on active service.[65]

The names of some of the Lysaght's workers who were killed in action with the Somerset Light Infantry were published in *Bristol and the War*. They include:

Private William Head, a worker in the construction department. He was aged 20, the son of Mr and Mrs George Head of 3 Ranelagh Street Redfield. He had been a choirboy at Christ Church Barton Hill. He was

62 M. Richardson, The Bristol Strike Wave of 1889-1890 Parts 1 and 2 (Bristol, Bristol Radical Pamphleteer nos. 21 and 22: 2012).
63 Ditto.
64 For information about the zinc industry in Belgium: http://reflexions.ulg.ac.be/cms/c_350208/en/the-saint-leonard-affair?portal=j_55&printView=true.
65 *Bristol and the War*.

killed at Hooge on 4th August 1915, in Flanders near Ypres. In the 1911 census he was listed as a 'rivet boy' in an ironworks, aged 15. George Head also worked at Lysaghts, as a storekeeper and labourer. William's older brother George was disabled; another brother Robert was a paint mill hand, and his sister Amy worked in a warehouse.

Lance Corporal Albert Trimnell, of 6th Battalion Somerset Light Infantry, was aged 24 when he was killed in action on 12th February 1916. He lived at 53 Roseberry Avenue Redfield. He had been a footballer with Dings A.C.

Private Edwin Butcher was 33 years old when he was killed on 18th August 1916 at the Somme. He lived at Haywards Road Barton Hill and had been wounded twice.

## Endnote

Alfred Jefferies is commemorated by a headstone in France; his brother Arthur's headstone is an area for those with no known grave. Commander in Chief Field Marshall Douglas Haig has been remembered with a statue at his old school, Clifton College in Bristol, and a prominent one in Whitehall London.

The First World War continues to provoke debate. We are, it seems, still loath to learn lessons from the conflict. Its outcome has had a significant effect on the Middle East to this day. One hundred years later, the horrors of war continue.

As the late Pete Seeger sang:

Where have all the flowers gone?
When will we ever learn…?

Workers at the Lysaght's wire factory, St Philips in the early 20th Century.

## Appendice
## Appendix A: The Jefferies family history

Arthur and Alfred Jefferies were born into a large family.

Their paternal grandfather, Isaac Jefferies, hailed from Siston, Gloucestershire. In 1851 he was working as a sugar boiler, living at John Street St Philips with his wife Sarah, son Thomas, daughter Sarah, and his brother William, a butcher. By 1871 the family had moved to Barley Fields in the Dings area. Isaac worked as a labourer in a flax factory, as did his son Leonard, aged 17. Isaac and Sarah Jefferies had four sons and four daughters.

Leonard Jefferies married Georgina White in 1874 and by 1881 they had moved to Kilkenny Street, St Philips. Arthur was born in 1883 and Alfred in 1886. They had two more brothers and four sisters. Leonard worked as a stationary engine driver. He died aged 42 in 1894.

By 1901 the family were living at South Parade, Freestone Road, off Gas Lane, in St Philips. Widow Georgina worked as a boot machinist, and her daughter Mabel in a tobacco factory. Arthur was a bottle maker and Alfred

Statue of Field Marshall Douglas Haig at Clifton College, Bristol (1950s).

a carter. Older brother William was a haulier. They had two sisters of school age, Beatrice and Mary.

Georgina Jefferies' large family grew further when her sons married. At the time of the 1911 census, Arthur and Alfred's older brother William was 33 and married to Julia. He worked at Lysaght's. They had a six year old son, also William, and lived at 4 Derby Street, St George.

In 1907 Arthur married his wife Marice. At the time of the 1911 census they had two boys, Arthur Leonard (2) and Edward George (11 months). Arthur was 27 and worked as a labourer in a glass bottle works. His family were staying with William Grandfield, a boot repairer, his wife and their three children. There was also a lodger, John Timmins and his son.

Georgina, her son Alfred (24) and daughters Beatrice (22) and Mary (18) had moved to 33 Edward Street St Phillips by 1911. Alfred, like his brother William, was working at Lysaght's as a galvanised iron worker, Beatrice was working in a tobacco factory and Mary was a box maker. Mabel was not listed and may have married. Older brother Fred had also married and moved from St Philips.

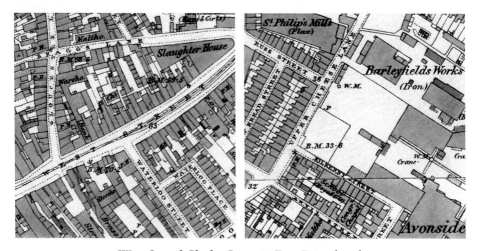

**West St and Clarks Court in East Bristol and Kilkenny St and Barleyfields Iron works (1880s).**

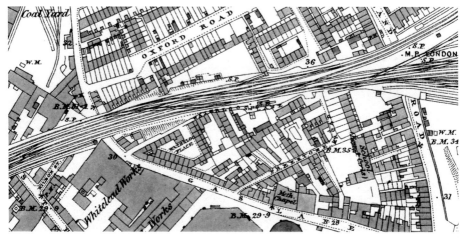

**Freestone Rd in The Dings (1880s).**

Alfred and Arthur's mother Georgina was the daughter of Fred White, a fly [horse carriage] driver, and Hannah White, a shoe binder. She was born in 1852 and they lived at Gloucester Place Cheltenham. By 1861 they had moved to Bristol and lived at Clark's Court West St, Old Market. Fred was listed in the 1871 census as a coachman. Georgina was 19 and working as a machinist. In early 1874, she married Leonard Jefferies. She lived at 33 Edward Street St Philips until she died in early summer 1937, aged 85.

# Appendix B: St Philips and the Jefferies Family

In 1861 Clarks Court, where Alfred and Arthur Jefferies' mother Georgina once lived, was a narrow passage off West Street. It was typical of many Bristol 'courts' of tiny dwellings with no facilities. Like most courts, it was demolished as part of street improvements. The area was developed in the 20th Century and is now the site of the Hide Market, opposite Gloucester Lane.

In 1871, Alfred Jefferies' father Leonard lived at Barleyfields, in the Dings area. He and his father Isaac probably worked at the St Philips flax Mill close by in Upper Cheese Lane. After Leonard married Georgina White they lived at nearby Kilkenny Street. The Barleyfields area housed an iron works, Avonside Engine Works, and the Jewish Burial Ground. This cemetery is still there and is off Barton Road. The current street named Barleyfields is a modern housing development.

The Jefferies' lived in Freestone Road in 1901. From Gas Lane the road now leads round to a foot tunnel under the railway from Temple Meads, leading to Oxford Street near the Dings Park. At the turn of the 20th Century the street was surrounded by heavy industry, including a large gas works. There were lead and vitriol works between Gas Lane and the river Avon. Freestone Road also had an early Board School and there was a nearby Methodist chapel.

A short walk away was Lysaght's Victoria works. A contemporary sketch by Samuel Loxton depicts this street and Lysaght's works.

The Victoria factory building still stands today, at the junction of Silverthorne Lane and Gas Lane.

In 1911 Arthur Jefferies and his family were listed in the census as visitors at Grafton St, which was close to Victoria Road near Feeder Road. Nearby was Stanhope Street.

Alongside the river Avon opposite Temple Mead station was the Phoenix Glass Bottle works. It's likely that Arthur Jefferies worked there. The works are now the site of Glass Wharf, opposite a footbridge from Temple Quay

**The Masons Arms on Stanhope St.**

In 1911 Alfred Jefferies was at Edward Street, in the Dings, close to the main railway line and engine sheds near Barrow Road Barton Hill. At nearby Folly Lane was a gas holder and works. Edward Street and other houses in the area were demolished in the 1970s. The area now houses light industry and the local council recycling depot.

The streets where Alfred and Arthur Jefferies lived have been demolished. There was a period of slum clearance in the early 19th Century, and the houses off Gas Lane were pulled down. They lacked bathrooms and inside toilets, were poorly constructed, damp and overcrowded. St Philips and the Dings was an area polluted by noise, smoke and fumes from heavy industry where their workers and families lived. The late 19th and mid-20th Century heavy industry has long since closed down, but the area remains one of light industry. Evidence of the past can still be found amongst the workshops around Gas Lane; some of the side streets are still cobbled.

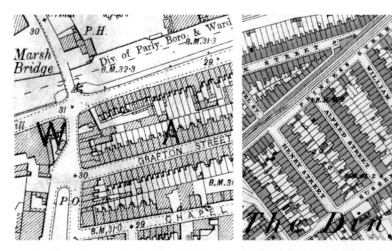

**Grafton St near the Feeder (1902-4) and Edward Street in The Dings (1880s).**

38

Victoria Road, St Philips; First World War memorial (1920).

# Bibliography

W. Allison and J. Fairley, *The Monocled Mutineer* (London, Quartet Books: 1979, reprint 1986)

A. Babington, *For the Sake of Example: Capital Courts-Martial 1914-1920* (Barnsley, Leo Cooper: 1983)

J. Belsey, *The Forgotten Front: Bristol at War 1914-1918* (Bristol, Redcliffe Press: 1986)

D. Bolton, *Made in Bristol* (Bristol, Redcliffe Press: 2011)

G. Braybon (ed.), *Evidence, History and the Great War: Historians and the Impact of 1914-18* (Oxford, Berghahn: 2003)

D. Geary, *European Labour Politics from 1900 to the Depression* (Houndmills, Macmillan: 1991)

C. Howell, *No Thankful Village* (Bath, Fickle Hill: 2002)

G. Oram, *Death Sentences passed by the military courts of the British Army 1914-1924* (London, Francis Boutle: 1998/2005)

J. Putkowski and J. Sykes, *Shot at Dawn* (Barnsley, Pen and Sword Books/Leo Cooper: 1989/99)

J. Putkowski, *British Army mutineers 1914-1922* (London, Francis Boutle: 1998)

M. Richardson, *The Bristol Strike Wave of 1889-1890 Parts 1 and 2* (Bristol, Bristol Radical Pamphleteer nos. 21 and 22: 2012)

E. Wyrall, *The History of the Somerset Light Infantry (Prince Albert's) 1914-1919* (London, Methuen: 1927)

**Midland Road-Unity Street junction, St Philips (1906).**

## Archives and other sources

Papers re the executions of Pte L Phillips and Pte A Jefferies: Somerset Heritage Centre Taunton ref DD/SLI/12/2/28a.

Trench War diary of the 6th Battalion of the Somerset Light Infantry: mostly written by Captain Adjutant R A Somerville. Taunton Heritage Centre; document reference DD/SLI/2/7.

Census records from www.findmypast.com.

National Archive online war records.

National Archive Field General Court Martial files.

The Bristol Directory (Wright's): Bristol Central Reference Library.

Bristol and the War: Bristol Central Reference Library.

Great Britain, The War Office, Statistical Abstract of information regarding the British Armies at home and abroad 1914-1920 (London: HMSO, 1920)

## Picture Credits

Front cover: The Shot At Dawn Memorial (2000) at the National Memorial Arboretum, near Alrewas, Staffordshire. Sculpted by Andy De Comyn. "The memorial was modelled on the likeness of 17-year-old Private Herbert Burden, who lied about his age to enlist in the armed forces and was later shot for desertion." - Wikipedia

Page 3: en.wikipedia.org/wiki/Recruitment_to_the_British_Army_during_the_First_World_War

Page 10: Barton Hill History Group